THE SUM OF US

by David Stevens

SAMUEL FRENCH, INC.
45 WEST 25th STREET NEW YORK 10010
7623 SUNSET BOULEVARD HOLLYWOOD 90046
LONDON *TORONTO*

IMPORTANT BILLING AND CREDIT REQUIREMENTS

All producers of THE SUM OF US *must* give credit to the Author of the Play in all programs distributed in connection with performances of the Play and in all instances in which the title of the Play appears for purposes of advertising, publicizing or otherwise exploiting the Play and/or a production. The name of the Author *must* also appear on a separate line, on which no other name appears, immediately following the title, and *must* appear in size of type not less than fifty percent the size of the title type.

Following productions at the Williamstown Theatre Festival and at A Director's Theatre in Los Angeles, *The Sum of Us* was presented for a long run at the Cherry Lane Theatre in Manhattan by Dowling Entertainment, et al., under the direction of Kevin Dowling, with sets by John Lee Beatty, lighting by Dennis Parichy, costumes by Therese A. Bruck, sound by Darren West, and stage management by Larry Bussard, and with the following cast:

JEFF .... Tony Goldwyn

DAD .... Richard Venture

GREG .... Neil Maffin

JOYCE .... Phyllis Somerville

CHARACTERS

HARRY MITCHELL.....................The father.

JEFF ....His son.

GREG...................................A young man.

JOYCE......................... A divorced woman.

The sitting room of a house in Footscray, and later, in the local park.

Footscray is an industrial suburb of Melbourne, Australia.

Scene 1

JEFF comes in from jogging, sweating profusely and gasping for breath. HE collapses on the sofa, takes off his footy shirt and mops his brow.

JEFF. I'm fucked.

DAD. (*Calls from the kitchen.*) What?

JEFF. I said I'm rooted.

DAD. (*Comes in.*) Stop off for a quickie somewhere?

JEFF. Ah, you're really off sometimes, you know? You put a dirty meaning on everything.

DAD. Wishful thinking, I suppose. How was practice?

JEFF. Not bad. George Papadopolis did his ham string.

DAD. (*Appalled.*) Will he be right for the game?

JEFF. Dunno. Coach doesn't think so.

DAD. But he's our best goal kicker, we'll be useless without him.

JEFF. Don't get your knickers in a twist, it's only a friendly game. Not like Footscray playing the Bombers, or anything serious. What's for tea?

DAD. All football is serious. Lasagna.

JEFF. Ah, not again.

DAD. It's that frozen one you like. With mashed potatoes and veggies.

JEFF. We've had it twice this week already.

DAD. I had a busy day at work, I didn't have time to dream up anything fancy.

JEFF. Monday we had lasagna, Tuesday meat pies, Wednesday lasagna, and macaroni cheese last night. Nothing too fancy in that lot. Why can't we have a nice leg of lamb, we haven't had a roast for yonks.

DAD. Things aren't so wonderful when you're in the kitchen you know, sausages and chips is a special treat when you're cooking.

JEFF. I did that nice chicken curry last week.

DAD. So hot it blew the roof of my mouth off.

JEFF. I'm sorry if you can't stand a little imagination in my cooking. I'll stick to frozen lasagna from now on. How long's it going to be, anyway?

DAD. Just about ready.

JEFF. I'll grab a quick shower then. (*HE heads for the door.*)

DAD. Why do you always decide to have a shower when I'm ready to dish up? Every time, just as I'm going to put the food on the table—

JEFF. You don't expect me to sit down all sweaty and smelly like this?

DAD. Doesn't usually bother you, unless you're going out. Are you? Going out?

JEFF. As a matter of act I am. Thought I might just pop down the pub for a beer or two.

DAD. You on a promise, or something?

JEFF. Can't a bloke even go out for a drink on a Friday night without you making a life time romance out of it? You dish up, I won't be two ticks. (*HE goes to have his shower.*)

DAD. He'll be back in a minute. (*HE starts to lay the table.*) He's a good lad, he's not usually on a short wick like this, but he's on edge about something.

(JEFF returns, wearing a towel around his nakedness, and socks.)

JEFF. (*Casually.*) You—um—you had a shower, did you then, Dad?

DAD. Yes. Yes, I did.

JEFF. You didn't turn the taps right off again.

DAD. Didn't I?

JEFF. Every time I go for a shower, the taps are dripping. I know you don't turn 'em right off because you think you're saving the washers, but that's what they're there for, and I'm a plumber, I can change 'em, that what I do for a living, and a few flamin' washers are a damn sight cheaper than the water rates. It drives me mental, Dad, you know it does, and if I've asked you once, I've asked you a thousand times, turn the fucken taps off!

DAD. Yes. Sorry. I will try.

JEFF. Thanks very much. (*HE leaves the room.*)

DAD. (*Starts dishing up.*) He's very wrought up, he only ever mentions that when he's wrought up. He must be meeting someone special. We'll know soon enough. If it's someone he's really keen on, if it's someone really special, he won't eat his pudding. I've got a Sarah Lee Blueberry Cheese Cake in the fridge, it's his favorite, but if he thinks he's meeting Mr. Right tonight, he won't eat any, and make some crack about breaking out in spots.

He's never been bothered by acne in his life, and I don't think it's going to start now, at twenty-four. You're probably wondering about what I said just now, about him meeting Mr. Right? Well, we might as well get it out in the open, as the actress said to the bishop, you're going to have to know sooner or later. He won't be meeting any girl tonight. He's what you might call—cheerful. I can't bear that other word. He's been like it since—well—since he was born, I s'ppose. I didn't want him to turn out that way, of course, but I think I always knew somehow. It's not as though he was ever a wimp or anything, any scrape, any adventure, even a punch-up, he was first in, last out, football was always his favorite game, and he's never liked pink as a color. So I think we both accepted the fact as a natural part of his life, and go on with living. Some of you'll be going tut-tut-tut, I suppose, but I don't really see why. He's a good, honest lad, with a heart as big as Western Australia, and he's as much a friend as a son. Mind you, he can be a nightmare to live with. Drives me screaming up the wall, sometimes.

(JEFF comes back from this shower. He's wearing jeans, and is taking a new shirt out of it's wrapper.)

JEFF. Didn't you take the washing in this morning? I haven't got any clean socks.

DAD. No, I forgot—I'll do it tomorrow—

JEFF. Ah, flamin' heck, Dad—

DAD. Well, you could have taken it in.

JEFF. What am I gunna do about socks? I can hardly go barefoot, not tonight.

DAD. You can borrow a pair of mine.

JEFF. I don't want to wear your rotten old socks.

DAD. Then whiz down the shop and buy yourself a pair of panty hose.

JEFF. Oh, ha ha, very funny. I s'ppose I could wash a pair of mine, and dry 'em in the oven. (*HE is putting his new shirt on.*)

DAD. The place'll reek of burnt nylon, like last time. What's that?

JEFF. What?

DAD. That shirt.

JEFF. It's a shirt.

DAD. It's pink.

JEFF. Yeh, Sort of.

DAD. You don't like pink.

JEFF. There's pink and pink. This is more like—warm white.

DAD. I never thought I'd live to see you in a pink shirt. Now come on, your dinner's ready.

JEFF. Two ticks— (*HE goes.*)

DAD. It's always the same when he's on a promise. He'll clean his teeth again, he'll change his jeans at least twice, he'll end up wearing my socks, and he'll come back reeking of Brut 33, by which time his dinner will be cold. Well, that's his problem. (*HE gets a book, sits at the table and starts to read, but then remembers:*) I wouldn't want you getting the wrong idea, though, two blokes living alone together, it's just him. I'm not that way inclined. Ladies man, that's me, always have been, always will be, I was a right little rooter when I was his age, Rabbit they called me. (*HE chortles happily at the memory, but then remembers his wife.*) Till I met his Mum, that is, no fooling around after that, I was faithful to her from the day I met her. Oh, there was the odd bit of flirting on the side, but nothing serious. It's not as though I didn't fancy other women, it's just, I knew when I met his Mum, that I was one of the lucky ones. I knew it was love. One day—Jeff had just turned ten—she went into town for the evening, with one of her girl friends, you know the way women like to get together and dish the dirt, and they were crossing the road, it wasn't that late, but there was this drunken hoon out of control in a car—I never even had the chance to say goodbye—(*The memory of it pains him.*) Jeff was only ten, and he's never talked about it, the way she died, but he won't drive when he's been drinking. Not ever. So it's just been the lad and me, and now we've got used to each other. There's never been another woman in my life since then. Up till recently, that is.

JEFF. (*Returns, dressed to kill*) You reckon these jeans are all right, or should I wear the dark ones?

DAD. How many pairs of my socks did you borrow, I can almost see your religion.

(JEFF, now in a fine humour, glances down at his crotch.)

JEFF. If you've got it, show it, I always say.

DAD. You haven't got that much to skite about.

JEFF. Yeh, well, size isn't everything, it's what you do with it that counts. (*HE goes into the kitchen.*)

DAD. (*Glances uneasily at the audience.*) His mother used to say that to me.

(JEFF returns with a dish towel, and ties it round his neck, after-shave wafting past Dad.)

DAD. What's that for, it isn't spaghetti.

JEFF. Don't want to get my new shirt dirty.

DAD. Yeh, marks show up on pink. You smell like a Bombay brothel, too.

JEFF. Good stuff, that, imported. Paco Rabanne. Cost a fair few bob.

DAD. Have you actually met this bloke yet, or is there some young man wandering around Melbourne who doesn't know that you're going to happen to him tonight?

JEFF. We've said g'day a few times, at the pub.

DAD. Ah, courting.

JEFF. Nah, not yet, anyway. Never know your luck, but. (*Smother his lasagna with tomato ketchup.*)

DAD. It's got tomato sauce on it already.

JEFF. I like more.

(THEY eat. DAD reading his book.)

JEFF. Good book?

DAD. Mmmmm.

JEFF. Course, some people think it isn't very good manners to read at the dinner table.

DAD. Some people haven't lived with you for twenty odd years.

JEFF. Some people should be so lucky.

(THEY eat. DAD reading his book.)

JEFF. What's it about?

DAD. Richard Burton.

JEFF. The film star?

DAD. There's more to life than what you see on telly, you know. Sir Richard Burton was one of the greatest explorers that ever lived. He was the first white man to see the Sacred Stone at Mecca, and the first man to discover the lakes in Africa that are the source of the Nile.

JEFF. (*Winks at the audience.*) I thought he married Elizabeth Taylor.

DAD. (*Sails on.*) He'd heard about this great lake, where the Nile came from, and after months of hardship in the heart of Africa, they'd all had malaria and dysentery, and diseases no one had ever heard of then, they were starving and just about to give up, but they were sheltering from the sun, and the native guide went on, up to the top of the next ridge, and started yelling, "Look, Master, look! Behold the great water." Behold—the great water! That stirs my blood that does, that shows you the power of words. A man who'd take on the whole world and conquer it. Not afraid of anything. You ought to read it, you might pick up a few hints.

JEFF. Whafor? I don't want to go chasing all over Africa looking for somewhere to have a swim, all them crocodiles everywhere. Anyway, it's all been discovered now.

DAD. No, it hasn't, you can still have adventures, all over the place, see things, do things. The outback, there's an adventure, you can still get lost there, my word, you can.

JEFF. I've been outback.

DAD. A ten day coach trip to Ayers Rock? It's not quite what I meant.

JEFF. You read too many books, that's your trouble.

DAD. You don't even have to leave home, there's amazing things waiting for you just around the next corner, if you only take the trouble to look, wonder things, like love, the greatest adventure of all. Your Gran said it once,

I've never forgotten it, the greatest explorers of all, she said, are the explorers of the human heart.

JEFF. (*Grins.*) Is that why she became a dike?

DAD. Your grandmother was not a dike!

JEFF. She was licking Aunt Mary's pussy for forty years, what else do you call it?

DAD. I admit her relationship with Mary was—intimate—but she was not a dike. Lesbian, perhaps.

JEFF. Lezzo, dike, what's the diff?

DAD. What's the diff, what the diff, there's a hell of a lot of flamin' diff! What's in a word, Shakespeare said, well, there's a whole bloody lot. Words give life to things, and meaning and beauty. Like your grandma was a very beautiful woman, and just because she found a bit of happiness after your granddad died, just because in her grief she turned to Mary and they found a bit of comfort in each other's arms, that doesn't give you the right to call her names. How would you feel if I went round calling you a fairy, or a pansy, or a poofter?

JEFF. You do, half the time.

DAD. Only when you upset me. Eat your veggies. (*HE goes back to his book.*)

JEFF. (*Turns to the audience.*) 'Strue. Granma was a dike. Well—a lesbian. She was a wonderful woman, though. I used to go down there for me holidays, and they were the best times. Wasn't anything flash, where she lived, a little weather board on the outskirts of town, where nothing worked right, and the plumbing looked like it was designed by Picasso. Obsessed with plumbing, Gran was. Maybe that's where I got the idea for going into the trade myself. And clean? Gran was always polishing every bit of wood work in the house, you'd get up in the morning, and she'd be there, polishing away, so there was a lovely smell about the place, like lavender floor polish, cripes, I haven't seen that in the shops for yonks. Reminds of a funny story—but, well, that's a bit off, I s'ppose.

In the evenings we'd play Ludo, or Snakes and Ladders or Tiddly Winks, I used to love those games with Gran. She used to keep an old Monopoly set hidden in the drawer, but Mary wouldn't let her play it, real strict, Salvation Mary was, and Gran too, but not as bad as Mary. Funny, int' it, someone as religious as Mary, going on about the devil and all his works, then jumping in the linen battlefield with Gran every night. Just goes to show, doesn't it? But I was staying there once, and Mary went out for the evening. Well, the minute Mary was out the door Gran whipped out the old Monopoly board and had it set up before you could say Ned Kelly, her eyes all glinting. Not a word to Mary, she said. I tell you, it was the best game of Monopoly I've ever played, like Gran and me were doing something really wrong, fire and brimstone stuff. Isn't it funny how ordinary mortal sin can be? First time I ever went to stay there, I was, oh, I dunno, six, maybe seven, and a couple of my cousins were there too, so I had to sleep on a spare bed in Gran and Mary's room.

And I remember, I can see it so clearly, waking up on the first morning I was there, it was still early, and looking across to Gran's big bed, an old brass bed it was, and there was Gran and Mary, tucked up in bed, wrapped up in each other's arms. Gran was snoring, I remember, and I lay in bed looking at them for, oh, ever such a long time, and it seemed—natural, somehow, I dunno. Like the most natural thing I'd ever seen. Like love.

She and Mary used to put the old uniform and bonnet on every Sunday morning, then they'd shove the roast in the oven and head off to the 11 a.m. at the Citadel. I'd have to go along too, coz Gran, she really believed it was the answer. So you'd join in the hymns, and shout out Salvation, and have a real good time. I remember once it was all going on, the band playing, and the Songstresses banging their tambourines, and everybody singing their little hearts out, and yelling Salvation, and it all got so exciting I went up and flung meself on the Mercy Seat. That got the old biddies clucking, I can tell you, just saved another soul for Jesus, everybody likes a bit of drama. I copped curry from Dad when he heard about it, coz he knew what had happened, he knew it didn't mean anything. I was only twelve. But they'd all wanted someone to do it and nobody was, so I did. I've always liked to do the right thing by people.

When we got back, the roast'd be ready, the little kitchen'd be all steamy and hot, with Gran banging on the taps to make 'em work, and making the gravy and carving the meat. Mary'd look after the veggies, that's all she ever did, she was a lazy cow. Boiled the life out of 'em for forty-five minutes. She never did like veggies and I think she was getting her own back on 'em. Afterwards Gran and Mary'd go upstairs to that big double bed, and do whatever they did. Pro'bly just slept, be too tired for anything else. You ever noticed that? When you're on with someone, well, it's always nice to play hide the one sausage, of course, but most of all, the nicest thing about going to bed with someone on a regular basis is when they just let you sleep. That's the bit I like, snuggled up all safe and sound in their arms. Not that I'm an expert on relationships, mind you, but it happened to me once, and it worked real nice. For a while. (*He doesn't want to remember that.*) I mean, you meet some blokes that treat sex like they're going twenty-seven rounds with Bruce Lee, but that wears me out. I don't see what it proves. Maybe that's why I've never had much luck in the romantic stakes. Maybe I haven't got a high enough sex drive. Maybe I'm a bit—ordinary. (*HE glances at his father.*) Or maybe it's him, there's such a thing as being too well adjusted. There's been a couple of times blokes have stayed here, stayed the night, y'know, and then in the morning he comes in, they're fast asleep in me arms, he comes in, taps 'em on the shoulder and says "Do you take sugar in yer tea?" It can be a bit unnerving, I suppose. So it could be him. More likely it's me. Maybe I am just a bit—dull.

(HE pushes his plate away from him. DAD stares at the plate.)

JEFF. What's your story, then, Dad? You going out tonight?

DAD. Thought I'd have a quiet night at home. There's a film on telly—

JEFF. You don't feel like going out?

DAD. Don't worry, I'll watch it in my room. The coast'll be clear.

JEFF. That's all right, then. (*HE slurps his beer.)*

DAD. You know how mad you get when I don't turn the shower taps off?

JEFF. Yeh, sorry, Dad, but it drives me up the wall—

DAD. No, don't you apologize. You see, every meal you ever eat, you always push your plate away from you when you've finished. Always. And I've told you till I'm blue in the face. But you always do it. Doesn't matter where we are, here, out, Buckingham Palace for all you care, you'd push your plate away there too. And it drives me mental.

JEFF. Yes. Well. If that's how you feel.

DAD. That's how I feel. There's a Sarah Lee in the fridge.

JEFF. No, ta, Dad. Don't want to go breaking out in spots.

(DAD glances triumphantly at the audience. JEFF collects the plates.)

JEFF. Fact I'm running late as it is.

DAD. Bit early, isn't it?

JEFF. You know what they say about the early bird.

DAD. Yes, but I don't think that's the sort of worm people had in mind when they said it. Don't worry about the dishes, I'll do 'em.

JEFF. Ta, Dad. I'll just—ah—clean me teeth. (*HE does a little hop dance of excitement and leaves the room.*)

DAD. See what I mean? He hasn't been this excited for ages, this one must be quite something. He's right about my mother, though, his Gran. She was only thirty-odd when my father died. He was killed at sea, and she went into great grief. Two years, she didn't go out, she didn't do anything, she seemed to have lost the will to live. Then she turned to God, in the form of the Salvation Army, and before you could say General Booth, she was going steady with this pretty little Songstress. Coz Mary was pretty, that was about the only thing she had going for her. Had a few labels on herself, did Mary. I can't think why. Her family were nothing, and she was a lazy slut.

JEFF. (*Toothbrush in mouth, comes back to grab his beer.*) You can hardly call her a slut, Dad.

DAD. Figure of speech.

(*JEFF grins and goes.*)

DAD. Next thing, Mum took her in as a lodger, in the spare room, but it wasn't too long after that when Mary was sleeping in the big double bed with my mum. I didn't realize what was happening for a long time, and when I did, I went right off. I thought it was an insult to my dad's memory. Because he was a man, all right, a man's man, a big, laughing, cheerful man. At least, that's how I remember him, but you never can tell, can you? He was a sailor, and you know what they say about sailors, a poke in every port. People were no different then than they are now, there were all sorts of shenanigans going on in the bedrooms of the world, only no one ever talked about it. Perhaps that's why I never seriously considered being unfaithful to my wife, Jeff's mum. Maybe I was trying to hang on to some sense of order.

JEFF. (*Returns, hot to trot.*) How do I look?

DAD. Have you used up that whole bottle of after-shave already?

JEFF. Bit fierce, is it? He said it was his favorite.

DAD. It's probably quite nice, in moderation.

(*JEFF is already in the kitchen, splashing water on his face.*)

DAD. Where are you meeting him, the Prinny?

JEFF. That's if he turns up.

DAD. I thought you had a date?

JEFF. Well—yes—no—not a date, I mean, it's just, we're gonna meet for a drink, perhaps, and knowing my luck.

DAD. Well, there's always plenty of others.

JEFF. This is different, Dad. He's something else, he's well, he's sincere, you know what I mean, genuine.

DAD. (*Sees the bright spark in Jeff's eyes.*) Then I expect he'll turn up.

JEFF. Hope so.

DAD. You've got to have a bit more faith in yourself, Jeff. If you were my son's friend, I'd be pleased it was you.

JEFF. Doesn't always work like that in the real world, Dad.

DAD. Better not keep him waiting, then.

JEFF. Too right. Well—cop yer—

DAD. —later. Have fun.

JEFF. Thanks, mate. Do me best. (*JEFF goes.*)

DAD. (*Watches his departure for a moment.*) He's twenty-four years old, and he's no virgin, that's a sure and certain fact, but he's carrying on like it's his first ever date. You might have noticed he lacks a bit of confidence about himself in the romantic stakes? Never understood that. He's a good enough looking lad, if you like that sort of thing. When he first started—doing it—he was into any thing that moved, just about. Then one day, a terrible thing happened to him. He fell in love. At first it was wonderful. I've never seen him so happy. But it didn't last all that long. The other lad, Kevin, oh, he was nice enough, but a bit flighty, training to be a Qantas steward or something. After a couple of months he moved on to greener pastures, went to Sydney, and it just about broke Jeff's heart. He got over it, to an extent, but I don't think anyone ever forgets their first love. I know I never did.

Still you can't live your life on memories, can you?

(HE glances at the clock, then takes a note from his wallet. HE goes to the phone and dials a number.)

Oh, hello, I'd like to speak to Joyce Johnson, please.

Hello, we haven't met, but my name's Harry Mitchell, and I've been givin your name by Desiree's Introduction Agency, you've maybe been expecting me to call?

I'm very pleased to meet you too. Please call me Harry.

Oh, I quite understand, it's the first time I've ever done this sort of thing, too.

(HE crosses his fingers. Joyce, at the other end, is clearly a talker.)

No, no, nothing like that, no. I'm looking for a long term relationship too, I promise you. Companionship's the most important thing.

You sound like a very cultured type of person, so I thought we might meet and have a meal together, somewhere quiet and classy, you know, so we can talk and get to know each other, my treat, of course.

I happen to belong to the Footscray Social Club, and they do a very nice smorgasbord on the weekends—

—yes, the Football Social Club.

It's a very smart dining room, actually, and there's dancing, proper dancing—

You would? Well, that's wonderful, Joyce. Why don't we meet there, neutral ground so to speak? Sunday, at what, half twelve?

No, it's my pleasure, I promise, I'm looking forward to it. Till Sunday, then? Bye.

(HE puts the phone down)

I don't know about this one, at all. "I'm not looking for a physical relationship in the first instance, you know." Well, I am.

She's the second one they've introduced me to, the first one was a bit of a disaster, too. Nice enough looking, but no brains to speak of, nothing upstairs, and I like a bit of chat as well. But you've gotta be patient, you can't expect a coconut every time.

Joyce. Nice name. She could have been a bit nervous, I suppose. She calmed down a bit, she sounded almost—mellow—by the end. Her voice was all sort of warm, like runny toffee. She's divorced. She probably hasn't been out with a real man for ages, and she was a bit on edge. She could be a right little humdinger, when you get to know her. Never judge a book by its covers, after all.

(HE does a little waltz with himself around the room.)

Underneath all that, she's probably gasping for it. Companionship, I mean. Harry, my lad, you could be on to a winner here.

(Then HE glances at himself in the mirror, and slicks his hair back.)

Oh, there's life in the old dog yet.

Scene 2

JEFF, bright-eyed and eager, comes in, and holds the door open for GREG.

JEFF. Dad? (*To Greg.*) Come on in, mate.

(GREG comes in. HE is nervous.)

JEFF. This is it, home, sweet home. Nothing flash, or anything, but—well—it's home. Beer?

GREG. Yeh. (*HE relaxes a little.*)

JEFF. (*Goes to the kitchen to get the beers.*) Make youself comfy.

GREG. It's a bit like our place. Same layout, nearly.

JEFF. Oh, sorry, dunny's first on the right, if you—

GREG. No, I was just saying. Where's—um—is your dad out?

JEFF. He'll be in bed.

(GREG's nervousness returns.)

JEFF. (*Comes back with the beers.*) He's got a telly in there, and he always goes to bed early, if he thinks I'm going to stop out, tom-catting. (*He could bite his tongue off for the last slip.*) Sorry, I didn't mean—

GREG. (*Whispering.*) Shouldn't we be a bit quiet, then?

JEFF. What for?

GREG. (*Still whispering.*) In case we wake him up.

JEFF. He won't be asleep, not yet. He'll probably come and say g'day in a tick. You want to meet him? I'll let him know we're back—

GREG. No! I mean—let's have our beers first—

JEFF. It's all right. I told you, he knows all about me, what I do, and who I do it with. I bring blokes back all the time—(*And could bite his tongue off for that one, too.*) Not that there's that many! Cripes, I should be so lucky. The thing is, Dad knows and he doesn't mind.

GREG. Well, if you're sure—

JEFF. Scout's honour. If they've got any left. (*HE winks.*) Well—come one, sit down—relax. (*HE sits on the sofa, and pats the space beside him.*)

(GREG sits.)

JEFF. That's more like it. Cheers, eh?

GREG. Yeh. Cheers.

(THEY suck on their beers. There is a little silence.)

JEFF. Real glad you turned up tonight. Wasn't sure you would.

GREG. I said I would.

JEFF. Yeh, but some blokes don't keep their word.

GREG. I know. Been stood up a few times myself.

JEFF. Cripes, any bloke that stood you up must need his head read. I really liked you, first time I saw you, down at the pub. Took me yonks to pluck up courage to say g'day.

GREG. I thought you weren't interested. I'd seen you there before. And in the park, too. I work in the park, sometimes, and I've seen you there, jogging, in footy gear. Those shorts look really sexy on you.

JEFF. (*Can hardly believe his ears. Someone thinks he's sexy?*) Ah. Just training. For the club.

GREG. You play footy?

JEFF. Just the local club. Amateur stuff. But it's a laugh.

GREG. (*Giggles.*) More'n a laugh, what I've heard. What goes on in those locker rooms.

JEFF. That's just talk. Everybody's trying to out-butch everybody else, in there. It's all spit on the floor and how many sheila's did you root last night.

GREG. But haven't you ever—y'know—with any of 'em?

JEFF. Nah, not really. Oh, they know about me all right. Crack a few jokes sometimes. They call me Baxter.

GREG. (*Laughs.*) Back's ter the wall, boys—

JEFF/GREG. —here comes Jeff!

(THEY laugh together.)

JEFF. You play any sport?

GREG. Swimming, I do a lot of swimming. It keeps me away from home a fair bit, I s'ppose that's why. All by yourself, in the water, no one to hassle you, no one to give you a hard time. Won a few medals too, at school.

JEFF. Don't you get on at home?

GREG. Mum's all right, but Dad's a bit tricky, always picking on me, finding fault with everything I do. He went through the roof when I got my job.

JEFF. Gardening, what's wrong with that? That's butch enough.

GREG. He reckoned it wasn't good enough for me, there wasn't any future in it, but I'm bringing home nearly as much money as him already. Mum wanted me to go to dancing classes once, ballroom dancing, she said it was a good way to meet people, but he wouldn't hear of it, no son of his was going to dancing classes, all the usual bullshit. It wasn't as if it was ballet, or anything. He's always been the same, ever since I can remember, whatever I wanted to do he'd say it wasn't good enough, or what would all his mates think. I don't know. That's why I took up swimming.

JEFF. Wouldn't mind seeing you in your speedos.

(GREG looks at him and they are both sexually tense.)

GREG. (*Grins.*) I'll show you later, I got 'em on now, if you wear your footy shorts.

JEFF. You're on.

(The tension holds, and THEY sip their beers again. JEFF leans back onto the sofa, and pulls Greg into the crook of his arm.)

GREG. What about the other teams? The other footy teams?

JEFF. You're just an old footy perve, aren't you?

(GREG giggles.)

JEFF. (*Worries about the image that he might be building up.*) Just coz they're big butch footballers don't make 'em Superman in bed, y'know. Half the time they're so buggered from training they just lie back and let the birds do all the work. An' I remember once a few of 'em had been up to Manila for a holiday, and of course they ended up in a brothel. Well, when Jacko Rymer came back, he was really shocked. He'd been with this really beautiful Asian chick, and she'd done everything, all over him like a Chinese gymnast, and he wasn't too keen on that. Said he kept dreaming he was with an Aussie girl who'd just lie there like a soggy cornflake.

GREG. *(Isn't so keen on having his illusions shattered.)* Is that what you like? Straightforward and wham, bam?

JEFF. Well—I dunno as how I'd win any gold medals, but—I like a bit of action—

GREG. So do I.

(THEY look at one another for a moment, then kiss lovingly.)

DAD. (*Comes in, wearing his pyjamas and dressing gown.*) Thought I heard voices.

(GREG, hugely embarrassed, leaps to his feet, and turns away, to adjust the front of his jeans.)

JEFF. Oh, for crying out loud, Dad!

DAD. Don't let me interrupt anything.

JEFF. Can't you ever knock?

DAD. To come into the sitting room? I was just going to get a beer. Anyone else?

JEFF. Yeh, ta. Two.

(DAD goes into the kitchen.)

JEFF. (*Moves to Greg. Sotto.*) Look, it's all right, I promise it. Just relax, Carry on like usual

GREG. But he must have seen us!

JEFF. Cripes, he's seen worse'n that before. (*And realizes that sounds terrible.*) This mate stayed one night—it was a while ago—and in the morning, well, we were both feeling a bit fruity, so we thought we'd have a wake-up session and Dad brings the tea right in the middle of it.

GREG. What did he say?

JEFF. (*Giggles.*) He said—he said—be careful of the sheets!

(HE breaks up. GREG is amused and a little shocked.)

JEFF. Well, it broke the ice.

DAD. (*Determined to impress, comes back with the beers on a tray.*) Aren't you going to introduce me?

JEFF. Sorry—Dad, this is Greg. Greg, this is me dad.

DAD. Very pleased to meet you. You can call me Harry. Or Dad, if you'd rather.

(HE sits on the sofa and pats the place beside him to indicate that Greg should sit there. JEFF sighs.)

DAD. Sit down, sit down, make yourself at home.

GREG. Thanks. Um—

DAD. (*Raises his glass.*) Well. Up your bum.

(HE drinks his beer. GREG chokes.)

JEFF. It's only a joke, mate. Dad's always making jokes.

DAD. Breaking the ice, that's all. Cheers.

JEFF. Like the sheets joke, I just told Greg that one, Dad. Tell him how it got started.

DAD. Oh, Gary might be embarrassed—

GREG. Greg—

JEFF. No, go on, it's a laugh. (*To Greg.*) You'll like this.

DAD. Well, you have to know Jeff's Uncle Eric to understand it really. Bit toffee nosed he is, my wife's side of the family, and he never really approved of Jeff's mum marrying me. Not that he had any cause to be stuck up. He's only Ministry of Works, but some public servants are like that. And drink? A man'd die of thirst in that house. You like the odd beer or a glass of wine, don't you, Gary?

JEFF. It's Greg, Dad—

DAD. All you got in that house was half a glass of tonic wine with your tea and a nip of ruby port for a night cap. Well, we'd been staying there for the week-end once, Jeff's mum and I, and I thought—I'll get you—I don't know how, but I will. So as we were leaving, we were walking down the path, it was a warm night and all the neighbours were out in their gardens, we walked down the path and they were being smart and saying "so nice, do come again," and I called out—I called out—"Thanks for having us. Sorry about the sheets!"

(HE and JEFF collapse with laughter.)

DAD. "Sorry about the sheets!" Top of my voice. So all the neighbours could hear.

JEFF. "Sorry about the sheets!" Can you believe that?

DAD. They didn't speak to us for a year.

GREG. Why? What happened to the sheets?

(DAD and JEFF exchange a tiny glance.)

JEFF. Well, it was a joke, you see—

DAD. Just like that time with you and the lavender floor polish—

(JEFF is immediately alarmed. HE glances at Greg, and at the audience.)

JEFF. Hey, steady on, Dad, that's a bit off, that is.

DAD. Is it?

JEFF. In company.

(HE nods at Greg. DAD twigs.)

GREG. Lavender floor polish? What was that all about?

JEFF. Ah, nothing, just a bit of a misunderstanding, you wouldn't be interested.

(There is a tiny silence.)

DAD. You live at home—um—

GREG. Yeh. Worse luck.

DAD. Don't you get on with your family? Greg.

JEFF. Greg's mum and dad don't know about him yet, Dad.

DAD. Oh, I see. That's a pity, don't you think, Greg? I mean, you're their son.

GREG. It's just—there's never been the chance.

DAD. I expect you could make the opportunity, if you really wanted to.

JEFF. Leave it, Dad—

DAD. I've always been very grateful that Jeff's been so honest with me. Not that I had a lot of choice, really, walking into the back shed when you were—what?—fourteen and finding you up Willy Jones's bum.

JEFF. I wasn't up his bum!

DAD. As near as dammit.

GREG. You're very broad-minded, Mr.—um—

DAD. I try to be, lad. After all, this is Jeff's home, if he can't be himself here, where can he be? And you think of this place as a second home, Greg. You're welcome here anytime you like. We don't have secrets from each other here.

GREG. (*Touched.*) Thanks very much, Mr. Mitchell.

DAD. Oh, none of that. Either "Harry" or "Dad." But I suppose that depends on how long you plan to go on seeing my Jeffrey, doesn't it?

(GREG gives a half smile of agreement.)

JEFF. Nothing on telly, Dad?

DAD. Nothing worth watching. This is much more fun. Family.

JEFF. (*Throws his eyes to heaven.*) I think I need another beer. Anyone else?

GREG. No, I'm right.

JEFF. You want something a bit stronger? There's some Scotch, and there might be a drop of brandy left.

GREG. Wouldn't say no to a drop of Scotch. (*HE relaxes a little.*) You know what they say. Whiskey makes you frisky.

JEFF. Yeh, and brandy makes you randy.

DAD. (*Can't resist it.*) Pity we haven't got any rum.

GREG. (*Laughs.*) That's a good one, I like that.

JEFF. Make it double then, eh? Just get the ice. (*HE goes into the kitchen.*)

(DAD sighs happily.)

GREG. Nice place you've got here, Mr. Mitch—Mr. M. I like that feature wall.

DAD. Thanks, lad. Getting a bit shabby here and there, needs redecorating. Get around to it one day. Was it busy, at the Prinny?

GREG. Yeh, packed.

DAD. Nice pub.

GREG. You've been there?

DAD. Oh yes. When it became obvious that Jeff was, you know, that way. I thought, well, it's his life, his heart. And since I'd never really met any Willie Woofters—sorry, I meant Gay Persons—not that I knew of, I thought I'd better try and find out what it was all about. I wanted to know who his friends were, I didn't want him to have to keep them secret from his dad. So I got him to take me on a pub crawl.

GREG. I think that's wonderful. Where'd you go?

DAD. Oh, we had a great time. I didn't realize there were so many places. I liked the Prinny best, a very nice crowd. We ended up at a disco at two in the morning, The Barracks, I think it was, all done up like a prison inside, and everyone wearing torn clothing. I thought it was a bit aggressive at first but then I got talking to these two blokes, nice lads, a bit nancy, but really good fun, and they called the place "Woman's World," that made me laugh, I can tell you, and I realized it was all a bit of a game. One of them—

(JEFF comes back with the ice, and pours the drinks.)

DAD. I think he must have thought I was that way inclined, too, because he asked me my name, and when I said Harry, he said, oh no, he said, that doesn't suit you, you'll always be Harriet to me.

JEFF. (*To Greg.*) This is funny, this is.

DAD. Well, it's not a name I've ever been fond of, reminds me of one of my aunts, on my dad's side, she was called Harriet, and a right proper bitch she was too, so I said "Harriet?" I said, "Harriet? Never. Call me Henrietta."

(GREG laughs and JEFF cracks up.)

JEFF. I heard him, clear as day. Nearly wet meself. Henrietta! Him! Can you imagine!

GREG. It doesn't really suit you.

DAD. Don't you think? I thought it was rather good myself, a bit refined, you know?

JEFF. One large Scotch.

GREG. Ta.

JEFF. Well. Here's to us.

(THEY drink.)

DAD. What do you do for a crust, Greg?

JEFF. He's a gardener, Dad.

DAD. Deaf and dumb, is he?

GREG. (*Laughs.*) I work at the council nurseries.

DAD. Is that fun?

GREG. Oh, it's great, they're a beaut bunch of people, very casual. Maybe it comes from looking after plants all the time, you can't hurry nature, after all, so it's not good getting ulcers because it's the middle of winter and the roses aren't in bloom. That's what I like about it, the plants just take their time, they rest in winter, and every spring they grow. Then suddenly, for a moment, they're beautiful. I don't think I've ever seen an ugly flower.

DAD. That's very nice, Greg—short for Gregory, is it? I see you appreciate the value of words, I wish you could drum some of that into Jeff's brain.

GREG. It's just the whisky talking, I expect. I'm a two pot screamer.

JEFF. I'm a bit like that myself. Two and I'm anybody's.

GREG. (*Giggles.*) Three, and I'm everybody's.

DAD. Four and I'm nobody's.

GREG. (*Very relaxed now. HE holds up his glass to Dad.*) Well—up your bum, Henrietta!

DAD. Up your dress, Griselda.

(HE and DAD think this is a great joke. JEFF can't help feeling that he's at the wrong party, somehow.)

JEFF. You two are well away, aren't you?

DAD. Tell me something, mate, what's your ambition, your dream? I mean, apart from playing hide the sausage with my Jeffrey, what would you really like to do in life?

GREG. My secret dream? My really, truly secret dream?

DAD. Have you got one?

GREG. Oh yes. (*His soul smiles a little.*) I'd like to plant a forest.

DAD. (*Thunderstruck.*) That is—magnificent.

GREG. Isn't it a beauty? You see, I met this bloke once, he was a violin maker, well, apprenticed to it, and he told me there's these famous violins made, oh, centuries ago, by some Stradvarious bloke, he used wood that was anything up to four or five hundred years old, and one of the reasons no one can make a violin as good as his is because they can't get wood that's old enough. All the forests being chopped down, the new trees aren't given time to grow anymore. That's when I got the idea. To plant a whole forest, and watch it grow, and stand in the middle of all the great trees and say, I planted this, I made this.

DAD. Do it! That's wonderful, eh, Jeffrey?

JEFF. (*Thinks that Greg could walk on water if he wanted to.*) My oath. Make a fair old swag of violins, too.

DAD. "A fair old swag of violins?" Haven't you got any respect for the English language?

JEFF. What's wrong with the way I talk?

GREG. I like it, it turns me on.

(*JEFF's chest swells about two inches.*)

GREG. Sorry, Mr. M—Harry—bit bold.

DAD. Please. Pretend I'm not here.

JEFF. Oh, yes, please.

DAD. Why don't you give the young man another whisky, Jeff?

GREG. No, I shouldn't.

JEFF. Go on, just a taste, freshen it up.

GREG. Well, this is really the last. I might do anything.

JEFF. Feel free. I'll get some more ice. (*HE goes.*)

DAD. (*Waits till the coast is clear, then fishes in the book cupboard.*) I'm very pleased you like my boy, Greg. He doesn't push himself enough sometimes, but he's got a heart of gold and he likes you.

GREG. I think he's very nice.

DAD. But—if you need anything to—well, he can be a bit of a lump sometimes—I've got these magazines—(*HE produces three gay porn magazines.*)

DAD. You know—if you need help—getting started—

GREG. Are these Jeff's?

DAD. No, I bought them. I wanted to find out what Jeff got up to. I had a pretty good idea, of course, but there's a few things in there I could never have imagined. And this one, it's all about safe sex. I was worried about this dreadful AIDS thing, who isn't these days, and I wanted to know if Jeff—if he was safe. He's my son, it's important to me. I left it lying about for him, so he'd know what do do, but he said he already knew about it.

GREG. It's all right, Mr. M., I do safe sex too.

DAD. Well, there you go, In case you need a turn-on. And—um—have a good time, won't you?

GREG. Yeh, ta very much.

(The conversation has made GREG reflective. JEFF comes back with the ice.)

DAD. I'll leave you to it, then. Very nice to meet you, Greg.

GREG. You too, Mr. M.

JEFF. You off, Dad?

DAD. Have to get my beauty sleep. Night, Jeff. Don't do anything I wouldn't do, you two.

JEFF. Dead set, Dad. Sleep tight.

(DAD grins and goes. GREG stares into his glass.)

JEFF. Can't believe he's gone to bed at last. Thought he'd never get the hint. (*HE comes back to Greg, and, a little diffidently, puts his arms around him.*)

JEFF. So—it's just you and me—

(DAD comes back into the room. GREG jumps away from Jeff.)

DAD. Oh Greg—I nearly forgot—how do you have your coffee in the morning?

GREG. Ah—as it comes—

DAD. White and two?

(GREG nods.)

JEFF. (*Moves to Dad and says, in a harsh whisper:*) Piss off, willya?

DAD. Don't mind me, I forgot my drink—night all—*(HE leaves.)*

JEFF. *(Tries to make the atmosphere congenial.)* He means well, but he can be the wrong kind of pain in the bum sometimes. Now—where were we?

GREG. Look—do you mind—I think I'll give it a miss.

JEFF. Ah, come on, it's still early—

GREG. No, really, I—'nother time, eh?

JEFF. He say something to you?

GREG. No. He's a wonderful man. It's just—I've—um got a bit of a headache, that's all.

(JEFF glances at the audience.)

GREG. Migraine—I suffer from 'em. Really blows you apart, y'know, y'can't think or anything.

JEFF. I've got some panadeine.

GREG. Doesn't help. I need these real strong ones, I've got 'em at home. I'd better push off. It's—um—been great—

JEFF. It's him, isn't it? Dad.

GREG. No—it's not him—it's not you or anything—it's just me. I can't hack it. Seeing you and your dad, I think it's terrific, it's how I'd like to be, bringing your boyfriend home and not having to lie, and pretend. I think it's terrific what you've got with him, I really do.

JEFF. But—?

GREG. It hurts a bit, makes me feel guilty about—what we do. Maybe it's too domestic. Sort of makes the atmosphere—I dunno—not very sexy.

JEFF. I've got a leather jacket, I could put that on. (*Softly.*) Or a pair of footy shorts.

GREG. It's too much like being at home. And I go out to get away from home. The thought of my dad coming into my room in the morning and finding you and me, well, just finding us in the same bed, we wouldn't have to be doing anything, he'd—he'd—

JEFF. What would he do?

GREG. He'd kill me.

JEFF. Probably not. My dad didn't. Oh, he gave me a right old rollicking, but I think that was the shock as much as anything, what me and Willy Jones were doing when he found us. Didn't speak to me for two days after. But nobody dies from that.

GREG. Another time, eh? I'd like to see you again, I really would. I like you a lot, you're a real nice guy. So's your dad. Tell him I said goodbye.

(JEFF doesn't speak. GREG moves to the door.)

JEFF. Don't go, mate. Please.

(GREG stops a little embarrassed.

JEFF. Dad'll be asleep soon, sleeps like a log, wouldn't wake for Gabriel's trumpet. It'll be like having the place to ourselves, I promise, I—I like you, mate, true dinx. I don't just mean sex, we don't have to do that if you'd rather not. But—I like you, as a person, y'know. Like in the pub, we talked about the same things, laughed about the same things. Even when we didn't talk, when we were just sitting together, I felt—comfy with you. Don't go, mate.

Please. We could just talk, get to know each other a bit. (*Moment.*) Wasting my breath, aren't I?

GREG. Sorry.

JEFF. No, I'm sorry.

GREG. See you then?

JEFF. Yeh, mate. Course.

GREG. I do like you, Jeff.

JEFF. Ta.

(GREG goes.)

JEFF. (*Stares at the door for a long time.*) Shit. (*Then HE remembers something.*) I went up to Sydney once, for a bit of a holiday, y'know, I thought maybe I'd have more luck up there. I mean with all those thousands of poofters in Oxford Street, you'd reckon there'd be one for me. Didn't really work, but. Didn't have much more luck than I do down here. I dunno what it is, Dad reckons I'm too shy. Well, maybe I am. Just takes me a bit of a while to get to know someone, specially someone I fancy. Anyway the point is, I went up by train, overnight, it's nicer on the train, I reckon, have a bit of a feed, and then meet a few people in the club car, and I've heard that some of those stewards on the train bang like the dunny door. Didn't happen to meet one, of course. Anyway, I was sitting in the club car having a few beers, and it was good fun, it's easy to strike up a conversation on a train, I find, coz you're fairly sure that most of the people you meet aren't putting on airs. You can't put on airs on a train, can yer, well, maybe on the Orient Express, but it's a bit difficult when you're rattling through Albury and the barman says "You right, sport?" Not exactly top deck, is it?

And there was this woman there, by herself—a lot of the people that travel on that train are by 'emselves it seems, maybe that's why I like it, coz I'm pretty much a loner myself, and there was this woman, she was—well, she wasn't going to see the right side of fifty again, maybe even sixty, and that's being kind, and she was done up like a dog's dinner. You see 'em sometimes, specially at the races. They're always dressed up to kill, they can hardly lift their hands because they've got so many rings on, and necklaces, and they wear make-up like you see in those old movies, about an inch thick and real red cheeks and too much mascara, and so much lipstick that they leave marks on all the cups and glasses they use, and their hair's always permed and crimped and dyed colours that God never intended for any human being.

They're always on their own, like she was. She was sitting there, mutton dressed as lamb, drinking gin and tonic, doubles, and she'd had a few. Well, she was plastered, really. Not that you could tell for a while, I mean the amount she put away I'd have been half seas over. But then suddenly it all started to slip, somehow, one minute she was sitting bolt upright like she had an iron corset on, and the next minute she was all wonky, and her glass was nearly falling out of her hand. Every so often she'd try and pull herself together, but then she'd slip again, she was too far gone. I couldn't take me eyes off her somehow. And then a big fat tear, just one, it sort of spurted out of her eye and started rolling down her cheek taking half the mascara with it. She was staring at the floor, and she just kept saying, "Oh, the agonizing pain of it all. The agonizing pain." Over and over again she said it. Suddenly she got up and left. She tried to keep her dignity, and ten out of ten for effort, but she sort of lurched along the carriage. Then the train jolted and she got thrown against the door. She must have hurt herself, and I suppose it was sort of funny somehow, but you couldn't laugh.

Oh the agonizing pain of it all. That's what she said. I've often wondered what she meant. But I suppose I know. She just wanted someone to talk to, to have a good time with, to laugh and get drunk with, and cuddle up to. That's all. Doesn't seem a lot to ask, does it? How can you be too bloody domestic for Pete's sake? What was he looking for, Superman with a ten-inch schlong?

DAD. (*Peeps in.*) You still up? Where's Gary?

JEFF. Greg. He's gone.

DAD. Well, I've heard of quickies but that must be some sort of record.

JEFF. No, Dad. We didn't—he didn't—

DAD. Oh, I see. Couldn't sleep. Thought I'd have another beer. You want one?

(JEFF shakes his head and holds up his whisky glass. DAD gets the message and pours a hefty slug of whisky.)

DAD. He seemed like such a nice lad, too.

JEFF. Yeh. Didn't he?

DAD. You be seeing him again?

(JEFF shrugs.)

DAD. Well—plenty more fish in the sea, eh? (*DAD desperately wants to help.*) What do you fancy for tea tomorrow night? Might get a leg of lamb, you've always liked a roast. And baked potatoes and a nice rich gravy. Oh, and don't forget to sort out your washing. I'll take it down the launderette in the morning. Have you ever thought of going to one of those introduction agencies, they've got 'em for blokes. Or there's that computer dating service in that magazine you buy.

JEFF. Not tonight, Dad, eh? Some other time.

DAD. Fair enough. Don't stay up too late, son.

JEFF. No, Dad.

(DAD goes. Moment.)

JEFF. She comes into my mind, from time to time. That woman on the train. (*HE sips his drink and stares into space.*)

Scene 3

It is Christmas. JEFF, who has been decorating the tree, is talking on the phone.

JEFF. Yeh, all right, put me down for ten bucks. Yeh, yeh, be in the post Monday. Merry Christmas. (*HE puts down the phone.*) Cheeee, that really gives me the tom tits, y'know.

DAD. (*Calls from the kitchen.*) Who was it?

JEFF. Ah, some missionaries wanting money for spastic blind dogs, or something. Y'don't mind once in a while, but these days it seems you've always got your hand in your pocket.

DAD. Just say no.

JEFF. Oh, that really gets their Jesus juices going, that does. And you know me, Dad, I can't say no to anyone. About anything, really. Those mince pies ready? I've got the munchies. *(HE goes back to decorating the tree.)*

DAD. *(Comes in with some mince pies, and sniffs the air.)* You smoking that funny tobacco again?

JEFF. Had a few puffs, Dad, yeh. It's Christmas, after all. You want some?

DAD. I haven't smoked any pot since—well, since I met your mum. She wasn't keen on it.

(JEFF has lit a joint and offers it to his FATHER, who shrugs.)

DAD. What the hell. It's Christmas. *(HE tokes.)* Not that I ever smoked that much, but in those days—killed many a good party, too. You'd go off somewhere on Saturday night for a rage, and everyone'd be sitting round zonked to the eyeballs, not moving or talking, except to say, "peace, man" every few minutes. The music was always good though. Sex and drugs and rock and rrrrrrrroooooooollllllllll! *(Of the joint.)* This is rather smooth, isn't it?

JEFF. It packs a bit of a wallop, later. Pass us the decorations, willya?

(DAD takes a rather bedraggled fairy from the box and passes it to Jeff.)

JEFF. Ah, not her again. I thought we were gunna ditch her.

DAD. Never. Your mother bought this the first Christmas of our marriage, just before you were born. I suppose some people would call that an omen.

JEFF. She's looking a bit tatty, Dad. We should get a star, or something.

DAD. Not as long as I'm alive. When I'm gone, you can do what you like, but your mother loved this. It was our first Christmas together, and you were on the way. We didn't have a lot of money to throw around, but we were determined to make the best of it. We went into town, and oh, we had such a day! You wouldn't believe the fun we had that day. Your mum looked bright and alive, so pretty, and full of you. I think I was the happiest man on earth that day. My heart hurt.

We had roast pork for Christmas dinner, that year. Not a leg, we couldn't afford that, a nice bit of loin. With crackling. Nobody could make crackling crackle like your mum. It was about the only thing she could cook, of course. Your mother was a wonderful woman, but she was a terrible cook.

JEFF. I miss her, Dad. I miss her like stink.

DAD. Not half as much as I do, lad. It isn't possible.

JEFF. Yeh, I know, mate. Sorry.

(THEY drink in silence.)

DAD. I tell a lie. Your Gran could make good crackling.

JEFF. Had enough practise with Mary, didn't she? (*HE gives a dirty chuckle.*)

DAD. (*Glares at him.*) I'll thank you not to make coarse comments about my mother.

JEFF. Ah, come on, Dad, just a bit of a laugh.

DAD. It's not an easy thing for a man to accept that his mother was doing it with another woman for forty years. I used to wonder what they got up to that could be so wonderful, that the love between them must be extraordinary if they were prepared to risk everything—what people thought about them, what they said about them—for love. That's when I started to think about blokes and other blokes, I'd never thought of it before, wasn't interested in it, but if what Mum and Mary had was so amazing, maybe it was the same for men, too.

JEFF. But you never tried it, Dad?

DAD. No. I couldn't bring myself to it somehow. I think it was the idea of hairy bums that put me off. Anyway, I met your mum. Then there was you. Ah, well, I thought, it's in the blood, just skipped a generation from my mother to you. And I made up my mind that no matter what, you were going to be your own man, and I knew I'd love you. (*A slow burning anger starts in him.*) So do it.

JEFF. Do what?

DAD. Be it. Be the man you ought to be.

JEFF. I am—

DAD. Sitting round here every night feeling sorry for yourself, getting stoned, when you should be out making some contribution to life, seeing the world, sewing your oats, falling in love, going mad, something wonderful—

JEFF. I make a contribution. I look after people's drains. That's a very important thing. Life would be pretty shitty without plumbers, I can tell you. (*HE laughs smugly at his own joke.*)

DAD. Not very romantic, is it? Not like planting a forest.

JEFF. Ah, fair go. I'm just me—

DAD. I know you are. I gave you that freedom. So go on, prove to me that the way I've brought you up wasn't wrong. Prove to me that my mother wasn't wrong, that what she found was wonderful, worth everything, all for love.

JEFF. It's not that flaming easy, it doesn't just happen to order. The choice is a bit more limited, for one thing. Well, maybe some places. San Francisco, all the blokes wear their dicks on their sleeves there, they reckon—

DAD. Ever thought of going there for a holiday?

JEFF. I don't want to live like that, Dad. I don't want to live in a world that begins and ends with being gay. I like having all sorts of people around and every sort of person there is. I like it at work or the footy when the other blokes rag me about what I am. I like knowing I can cope with all that. And I don't want to live in a world without women. I like women. Me and the girls at the office get on great. I've even fancied some of them, done it with a couple of 'em, just to make sure I wasn't missing out on anything.

DAD. (*Deeply shocked.*) You've done it with girls? You've never told me!

JEFF. Yeh, well, I didn't want to get your hopes up.

DAD. Did you like it?

JEFF. See what I mean?

DAD. But was it all right, I mean, oh, bugger it, you got it up?

JEFF. Course I did, it's not exactly an obstacle course, not once you're in the cot. Quite enjoyed it, actually, something different. But they just don't turn me on like blokes do. They're a bit too soft and squashy for me. And they think different to blokes.

DAD. Wouldn't you like to try it again?

JEFF. No, Dad, not off the top of me head. That's what I mean about getting your hopes up. I like doing it with blokes, Dad, and I don't think it's ever going to change, because I don't want it to. But I don't want to be limited by other people's ideas of who I am, yours, or anyone else's.

DAD. I didn't think I've ever tried to put limits on you, Jeffrey.

JEFF. No, Dad, I know. I didn't mean—you've been beaut, mate, the best dad in the world, I reckon, the fairest, that's a certain fact. I don't often say it, but it's Christmas and I'm a bit stoned, so, well, thanks, mate, for everything. You give me the first class shits at times, and I suppose I do you, but I don't think there's many got a father like you.

DAD. And I've been a very lucky man to have a son like you. (*HE can't resist it.*) But there's gotta be someone out there fancies you, surely? That young Gary, he seemed keen enough—

JEFF. Greg.

DAD. You ought to see him again. Ring him up.

JEFF. I have seen him—couple of times—at the pub. Quite a few times, actually.

DAD. And?

JEFF. And what?

DAD. Well—have you asked him out? Taken him to the pictures, or a walk in the park? I don't know how these things work out between blokes, but you know, chatting him up, courting—

JEFF. I can look after that side of my life, Dad—

DAD. Haven't done too bloody well at it up to now. You need a poker up your bum.

JEFF. (*Grins.*) Don't think I'd fancy that.

DAD. (*Grins too.*) Perhaps not. But take him out for tea, somewhere nice, somewhere splosh. Y'know, candle light and soft romantic music, good tucker and a few bottles of wine. That'd soon open his legs.

JEFF. (*Shoots a look of apology at the audience.*) Ah, you're really off sometimes, you know that? How can I, after what happened here before—gave me the brush off then, dead set he did. Be a right galah going back for more of the same treatment, wouldn't I?

DAD. If at first you don't succeed. Grab the chance, rush him off his feet. Get him away from his place, get him away from here, from me. If you're short of a few quid, I can lend you some. It'd get you out of my hair for a weekend, at least.

JEFF. All right, stuff you then, if that's how you feel. I'll do it.

DAD. Have you got his number?

JEFF. Yeh, as a matter of fact I have.

DAD. Call him, do it now.

JEFF. Yeh, well, next time I see him, maybe tomorrer—

DAD. Don't say that!

JEFF. What?

DAD. Tomorrow, I'll do it tomorrow, that's been the story of your life, my boy, always putting off till tomorrow what you should have done today. Well, you're in for a very rude shock in the not too distant future, because one day you're going to wake up and it will be tomorrow, and there won't be too many other damn tomorrows left. And the rest of your life is like a whole lot of yesterdays, the past, all those wasted days of your life are gone in the blinking of an eye, like some half forgotten dream. Do it now, boy, whatever it is, don't put it off till tomorrow, because suddenly you'll find that you're old and wishing it was yesterday and all you'll be left with is a terrible regret that you didn't make a bit more of your life. It's very hard work being tolerant about you, sometimes.

JEFF. Being like me is hard work, sometimes.

DAD. Being anybody is hard work sometimes.

JEFF. Now, put a sock in it, Dad! I'm me, just me, that's all, whoever that is. You reckon you made me, well, all right, you've got to put up with me, the rough and the smooth. I want to fall in love again, dead set I do, I want that more'n anything. And I'm scared of it, too. I don't want it to hurt like last time, but if that's the price I've gotta pay, well, all right, but please, let it happen soon. I know I've got you, and all my mates, and everything, and that's great, but there's a part of my heart that's empty, Dad, and it's a very important part. I know you're a bit disappointed in me sometimes. I'm not one of your big explorers, discovering new countries, I'm never going to win any cups or prizes or be rich and famous. I'm never even gonna win Lotto, with my luck. And I'm never even gonna give you grandchildren, which is the least that most blokes can do. But I'm trying to do the best I can. And I'm sorry if that's not good enough for you, then I'll find somewhere else.

DAD. Oh, don't be daft, you silly bugger. I just want you to be happy.

JEFF. (*Still somewhat angry.*) I am happy. Sort of.

DAD. Oh, I hope so, lad. I hope so. That's all I've ever wanted for you, really. After you were born, the first time I'd seen you, held you, I walked home from the hospital, it was late at night, dark, and it was raining a little, but I didn't care, my feet weren't even touching the ground. I saw a church, and I thought, why not? My heart was so full, I wanted to share it with someone, even someone who might not really be there. Of course it was locked. Funny thing about churches, you can never get into them when you really need them. But there was a little seat in the porch, so I sat there and said a little prayer for you. Let him be anything, God, I said, let him be anything in the world that he wants to be. But let him be happy.

JEFF. I dunno if I believe in God, Dad.

DAD. I didn't once, but being an atheist is very hard work, you know. Your mum always used to say that. I don't know what I believe in, she said, but I'd rather believe in something than in nothing. And it's a nice idea, sometimes, it helps, sometimes. I think about her sitting up there on a fluffy white cloud in a place called paradise, surrounded by lots of fat little naked babies sprouting wings on their backs and angels with harps making pretty music, waiting for me to come and join her, and it helps. Sometimes. And sometimes it makes it worse. Sometimes I miss her so much, I can hardly wait to hear that pretty music.

JEFF. You ought to take a leaf out of your own book. Must be a few old widows floating round.

DAD. There's a few young ones, too.

JEFF. No, Dad. I mean well, I'm sure there's some as fancy you.

DAD. Would it worry you if there was?

JEFF. Bloody hell, no, it'd be great.

DAD. There is.

JEFF. You old dog! How long's this been going on?

DAD. (*Looking impossibly smug.*) A few weeks.

JEFF. You're lower than a snake's belly, you are. Not a word to me about it.

DAD. Don't go getting all hurt, I wanted to be sure.

JEFF. Well, this calls for a celebration. Where'd you meet her?

DAD. I—um—went to one of those introduction agencies.

JEFF. Dad—

DAD. You're not the only one gets lonely, boy, there's part of my heart that's empty too. I'm a man who likes women, I like the talk you can have with a woman that you can't have with men. I love the way they think, it's like a language you think you know but every so often you miss out on a few words. They drive me screaming up the wall, sometimes, but then so do you, sometimes. I like looking at women, I like their shapes. I like the way they're put together, I like 'em all soft and squashy, I like having them, for Pete's sake. I'm sick of living in sin with my own right hand—

JEFF. Easy, Dad—

DAD. What's up, that shouldn't worry you, you're going for world championship whack-off artist, aren't you?

JEFF. (*Glances uneasily at the audience.*) Sorry about that, it must be the dope, he's not used to it, he's getting a bit carried away, got the chats, or something. It's not quite like that. I mean, I do it, course I do, who doesn't? Gotta relieve the tension somehow, but he makes me sound like some rampant sex maniac. And you don't like to think of your own dad doing—that—do you? I mean, you know he must, but it doesn't seem quite right.

DAD. I was beginning to give up hope, they'd introduced me to a dog first up. Joyce doesn't know that, of course, she thinks it's first time lucky for both of us. She's a wonderful woman, Jeffrey. My side of forty, of course, and her hair's a bit violent, but she's still got her figure, and she's a lovely personality. And a very generous nature.

JEFF. (*Gives a small, dirty chuckle.*) You—um—you know, done it then?

DAD. You dirty little bugger.

JEFF. I thought you must have got into her knickers.

DAD. Don't talk about Joyce that way, if you don't mind. She's a very refined type of person.

JEFF. Well, I'll be—you old dog.

DAD. She's quite a catch, actually, I was worried about it being disloyal to your mum, to her memory, to bring someone else into her bed. But I think she'd understand.

JEFF. Is it love, then, Dad?

DAD. No, Jeff, I can't honestly say it is. It might be the next best thing, though. Do you mind? I've been worried about you.

JEFF. Me? Why me? I'm right. I don't come into this. (*He thinks he understands.*) Y'mean, you want me to move out or something? Course I would. Give you two a bit of space.

DAD. No, Jeff, this is your home, I wouldn't want that, nor would Joyce. She knows all about you.

JEFF. Oh, yeh?

DAD. She knows who you are, and that you live here, and all.

JEFF. Yeh, but you haven't told her everything, have you?

DAD. No, not that, not yet, there didn't seem to be any need. Let her meet you and get to know you a bit first.

JEFF. Come on, Dad. It's going to be hard enough for her coping with you, without your poofter son hanging round.

DAD. Joyce is a warm, understanding woman, you'll love her, you'll see. And if it all works out, because it will, you'll stay here, in your home, till the day comes when you want to move out. On your own. With someone.

(There is silence, while JEFF digests this.)

JEFF. When's the big day?

DAD. I haven't actually got round to popping the question yet—

JEFF. But you're going to?

DAD. I think so, if you two get on.

JEFF. It's your life, Dad, you do what you want, what makes you happy. (*HE chuckles again, and raises his glass.*) Well, I'll be—you old—Merry Christmas, Dad.

DAD. (*Raises his glass too.*) Merry Christmas, son.

(THEY sit there, each lost in his own thoughts, sipping the whisky, and munching contentedly on mince pies.)

DAD. Are we going to have another joint? (*Ripped beyond redemption.*)

Scene 4

It is night. The front door opens, and there is some giggling.

JOYCE. Harry, don't be silly, stop it. I'm too heavy, put me down.

DAD. Nah, dinkum, come on—

(DAD manages to carry JOYCE over the threshold, then puts her down, gasping a little. BOTH of them are in high spirits.)

JOYCE. It's a wonder you haven't done yourself a mischief.

DAD. I wanted to make you feel at home.

JOYCE. I'm not sure it isn't bad luck, you're only supposed to do that when you're married.

DAD. Life's what you make it, it's not a matter of luck. Well—here we are. Home, sweet home.

(HE has turned some LIGHTS on. JOYCE looks around appreciatively, but clearly with a re-decorator's eye.)

JOYCE. It's lovely, very comfy. You keep it nice and tidy, too, considering.

DAD. Jeff and I had a bit of a cleaning up session today. It isn't always like this.

JOYCE. Hardly likely, two men living alone. That feature wall's interesting. Colourful.

DAD. I thought so. Jeff wanted something plainer, but I stuck out for this.

JOYCE. No, it's got character. Makes the room a bit heavy, perhaps.

DAD. It needs a woman's touch. I'm sure you could do wonders with it.

JOYCE. (*Pleased.*) I must say, you know how to say the right things to a woman, Harry.

DAD. Life without women would be like a day without sunshine. Or a barbecue without any beer.

JOYCE. You've had a bit too much to drink already, if you ask me.

DAD. The night is young, and I've got some Irish Cream.

JOYCE. You didn't get it in specially for me, did you?

DAD. Well—Jeff and I don't drink a lot of it. (*HE decides to push his luck.*) Though he likes the occasional Orgasm.

JOYCE. What?

DAD. (*And wonders if he's pushed it too far.*) Irish Cream and Cointreau mixed. Very popular, he says.

JOYCE. Sounds like a bit of a lad, your Jeffrey. (*Giggles.*) I've never had an Orgasm before.

DAD. We can soon fix that!

(HE organises the drinks. JOYCE explores the room, looks at photos.)

JOYCE. It's been a wonderful evening. I haven't had so much fun in ages.

DAD. It isn't over yet.

JOYCE. Is this your wedding photo?

DAD. Oh—sorry. I meant to put it away.

JOYCE. Because of me?

DAD. Didn't seem very tactful, not on your first visit here.

JOYCE. No point in hiding the past, we've both got our memories, and they're important. She was a lovely looking woman, your wife. And you cut quite a dash. Is this Jeffrey?

DAD. On his twenty-first.

JOYCE. Mmmm. It's a wonder some girl hasn't snatched him up.

(Her comment might not be as innocent as it sounds. DAD flicks the merest glance at the audience.)

DAD. Yes. It's a wonder.

JOYCE. Playing the field, I suppose. Still, he shouldn't leave it too long, you men get very set in your ways.

DAD. I—um—suppose he hasn't met the right person yet.

JOYCE. Not through lack of choice, I'd say. He takes after his dad in the looks department.

DAD. Do you think? Oh, I don't know—most people say there isn't much resemblance.

JOYCE. Some people can't see the forest for the trees.

DAD. Or the bald head for the hair. One Orgasm coming up.

JOYCE. (*Giggles.*) It's a very rude name for a drink.

DAD. To us?

JOYCE. To us.

(THEY drink.)

JOYCE. Oh, yes, very smooth. I could get quite fond of those.

DAD. I hope you do, my dear.

JOYCE. I must say, this has all been a bit of a shock to me, us getting on so well. A very nice shock, I might add. I didn't have very high hopes when I went to the agency. It seemed a bit—degrading—to have to go looking for a man. But perhaps there are a few things we should sort out—now things seems to be getting a bit serious.

DAD. They are on my side.

JOYCE. How serious?

DAD. I want you to meet Jeffrey, and if you two get on, well, I'm going to pop the question.

JOYCE. And if we don't?

DAD. We'll cross that bridge if we have to. He's been talking about moving out, anyway.

JOYCE. It's a big step, all the same, and I'm more wary these days, there's more to consider when one marriage has failed on you.

DAD. He left you, it was hardly your fault.

JOYCE. Of course it was, part of it. You can't put all the blame on one side when a marriage breaks down, however much you might want to. We just got older, that's all. So when that floosy battered her eyelids at him, he was a sitting duck. She wasn't a floosy, I shouldn't call her that. She was quite a nice woman, actually, but she was young, and she made me look old. And that hurt, that hurt more than anything. Of course, it didn't last, I told him it wouldn't, but that didn't seem to make any difference to him. You're probably right, he said, you usually are, but I don't care. I want the chance, whatever happens, I want my freedom. Well, he's got it, and I hope he's happy. With her he was a silly boy all over again, a young ram sowing his oats, and he hadn't looked at me that way for a long time, I can tell you. Oh, we still—you know—did it, but it was habit as much as anything, like doing the dishes or feeding the cat. But I've got my needs too. Like you have.

DAD. Oh. Um—

JOYCE. You probably think I'm a bit bold coming right out and talking about it, but it's best we put our cards on the table. I may not be very imaginative in the bed department, Harry, I'm not keen on all the sexual gymnastics you read about in the magazines these days, but I never said no to him, not all the years we were together.

DAD. (*Intrigued, of course, but tries not to show it.*) Not once?

JOYCE. Well, obviously, there were certain times, after my daughter was born, and when I wasn't well. But apart from that, he always got his onions, whenever he wanted them. (*Giggles.*) He could have had 'em a bit more if he'd played his cards right. I like to be wooed.

DAD. I'll remember that.

JOYCE. So as long as you're not too demanding, you'll get what you want on that score.

DAD. You're a very generous woman.

JOYCE. Are you?

DAD. What?

JOYCE. Very demanding?

DAD. Oh—ah—I've no idea. I've never really thought about it.

JOYCE. Like hell you hadn't. (*SHE looks for a little Dutch courage.*) I wouldn't mind another one of those what'dy'call'um.

DAD. Orgasms.

JOYCE. (*Giggles.*) Couldn't quite bring myself to say the word.

DAD. I think it's time we stopped beating around the bush, Joyce—

JOYCE. I didn't think I was.

DAD. Let's not waste any more time, we haven't got enough of it to waste. (*DAD gets down on one knee.*) You don't have to give me an answer now, but you know what's on my mind. I've told you that already. So I'm going to ask you. Will you marry me?

JOYCE. (*Looks at him for a long moment. Then SHE starts to cry.*) Oh, Harry—

DAD. Come on, what's all this, what's there to cry about?

JOYCE. I'd given up hope. I didn't think—I didn't think it was ever going to happen to me again.

DAD. No. Neither did I.

JOYCE. I've been so lonely, for so long. And I didn't think it was ever going to happen to me again. (*SHE recovers a little, and smiles through her tears.*) It was you kneeling down that did it.

DAD. Well? Will you?

JOYCE. No.

DAD. Why? I thought—

JOYCE. It's too soon! I don't want to make another mistake. Let's give it six months, see how we go, see how I get on with Jeff, and if we still feel the same way then, I'll say yes.

DAD. Let's make it three.

JOYCE. It's all that talk about the other just now, about s.e.x. isn't it? It's got you all worked up, you're just after my body.

DAD. I can't say I find it unattractive.

JOYCE. It's manners to wait till you're asked.

DAD. I thought I did!

JOYCE. All right. Three months.

DAD. Oh, Joyce—

(HE kisses her. JOYCE responds. Then DAD looks at her fondly.)

DAD. I won't say I'm the happiest I've ever been, but I'm as happy as I can remember for a long, long time. (*HE kisses her again.*) I put a bottle of bubbly in the fridge, just in case—

JOYCE. You wicked thing, you had this all planned.

DAD. Never know your luck in a big city.

JOYCE. Thought you didn't believe in luck?

DAD. Perhaps I've changed my mind. You make youself at home. (*HE waltzes off to the kitchen.*)

JOYCE. (*Looks at the room that she hopes will one day be her home. SHE plumps a cushion, adjusts an ornament.)* How keen are you on that feature wall?

DAD. Oh, well, the place could stand redecorating.

JOYCE. That's another thing we'll have to talk about. What do I do with my place?

DAD. Rent it out. Be a nice little income for you.

(JOYCE picks up a book, then sees magazines in the book cupboard. SHE picks one up, then stares at the one beneath it.)

DAD. There. Didn't take long. What shall we drink to?

(JOYCE hides the magazine behind her back, as DAD returns, with glasses of champagne and a glint in his eye.)

JOYCE. Well—nothing—not quite yet.

DAD. What's wrong?

JOYCE. Isn't there something you should tell me first?

DAD. Like what?

JOYCE. (*Holds out the magazine.*) Like what these magazines are doing here.

DAD. Oh. Um. Well—That one's about AIDS—

JOYCE. More like a "how to get it manual." What are they doing here?

DAD. To be honest with you, I bought them.

JOYCE. Let's be real honest then, eh, Harry? Unless you're the sort of bloke that needs these things as some kind of turn on, that only leaves one other person, doesn't it?

DAD. I suppose it does.

JOYCE. I see. Somehow I think I guessed. I've been wondering why you never talk very much about Jeff's personal life, why he hasn't got a girl, or anything. But then I thought you would have told me, so I must be wrong.

DAD. I should have told you. Tomorrow, I kept saying, I'll do it tomorrow.

JOYCE. Why couldn't you have been honest? (*SHE almost breaks, her disappointment is so intense.*) Oh, why didn't you have the guts to tell me before? Are you ashamed of him, or something?

DAD. (*Looks at the audience.*) What can I possibly say? I've never been ashamed of Jeff, not ever. Disappointed, yes. Disappointed that he'll never find a girl and settle down. Disappointed that he'll never give me a grandson. Disappointed that my family's name will stop with him. And disappointed because I honestly think he's missing out on something—wonderful. I can't believe in my heart, that what my mother found with her girl friend, or what Jeff might find with any bloke, is a patch on what I had with his mum. I believe it can be love, I know it can, I know Jeff's been in love, I watched him and I saw the pain, and I knew that it was love.

But what I had with his mum, the life we shared together, the rows and the good times, the struggles and the fun, and most of all, making him, making a baby, knowing I'd put the seed in there and watching it grow, and then seeing him—

I couldn't believe it—that we'd made this thing, his mum and me, this little, tiny, living thing, and I wanted to hold him in my arms forever, take him away somewhere, him and his mum, and keep them safe from the rest of the world. And watching him grow, and the relief when everything turned out all right, he could see and hear and talk, he wasn't retarded or disabled, and fretting about him when he was sick, and being angry with him when he was naughty, and teaching him, and dreaming dreams for him. That more than anything. The dreams of what he might become. I remember the first time he went to school, he didn't seem old enough, he didn't seem big enough to be setting out on such an adventure, but he was a cocky little shit, all set to take on the world. But the night before, I was tucking him into bed, and I kissed him, and he whispered to me, he said, is it going to be all right, Dad, at school, am I going to manage? It nearly broke my heart. And I remember so many things.

So yes, I'm disappointed that he won't ever experience those things, because I think they're important, I think they're what life is. But if he's never going to have those things then I want him to have all the things he can have. If he was a liar, or a thief, or a murderer, maybe that would be different, though I don't think so, he'd still be my son. But Jeff is a kind and generous man, and no one can deny that he is honest. Our children are only the sum of us, what we add up to. Us, and our parents, and our grandparents, and theirs and all the generations.

(HE turns back to Joyce.)

No, Joyce, I'm not ashamed of him. I made him. How could I be ashamed of what my seed has become?

JOYCE. *(Calmer now.)* You should have told me, Harry. It's not just that you know about it. You accept it. You encourage it.

DAD. It doesn't change anything between us, Joyce.

JOYCE. *(Cries from the heart.)* It does! You lied to me, and let me fall in love with the lies!

DAD. Please, Joyce, just meet Jeff. You'll love him, you'll see.

JOYCE. I can't, Harry, I've met a couple of the gay boys, nice enough, I'm sure Jeff is too, but I can't imagine how they can do what they do. The thought of two men, touching, doing what they do—or two women—it makes me—and I know it's not fashionable, but that doesn't help, it's how I feel, and what I know doesn't help how I feel.

DAD. Then what are we gunna do?

JOYCE. You said he was going to move out. That he was talking about it, anyway.

DAD. (*Immediately on guard.*) Don't make me choose, Joyce, please.

(Moment.)

JOYCE. No. Well, perhaps not.

DAD. Joyce—(*HE embraces her.*) He'll probably be home by midnight—

JOYCE. No. Not tonight. It's too soon. I couldn't—it's not just him, it's everything. I need to be alone, I need to think about it, sort it out in my head. I couldn't handle it right now. (*SHE gets her coat.*) It's been great, Harry. Like a walk on a beautiful evening.

DAD. Don't go, Joyce, please—

JOYCE. I have to. I'll see you, Harry.

DAD. When—?

JOYCE. A day or three. I've got your number. I'll give you a call. (*SHE goes.*)

DAD. (*Stands by himself for a moment and stares at nothing. Then HE smiles a little, remembering a time when he was happy, and gets his champagne.*) Up your dress, Henrietta!

Scene 5

The park. A sunny day.

JEFF is sitting on a bench, reading from a book, two or three other books beside him. DAD is nearby, in a wheelchair.

JEFF. . . . and the Arab shouted "Look, Master, look. Behold, the Great Water. (*HE look up from the book.*) "Behold, the Great Water." That's pretty neat, isn't it? Makes it sound really something, after all the adventures they'd had. That's one good thing these last few weeks, Dad, reading your books to you, it's opened my eyes. I can tell you. You all right, anything you need?

(DAD buzzes a BUZZER on the arm of his chair.)

JEFF. Ripper day. Weather report on the telly last night said it was going to rain, still, they don't get it right very often.

Could be a good summer, that bloke does those long range predictions reckons it will. I was thinking about summer holidays, if you'd like to go somewhere, not very far, of course, it's a bit tricky with the wheelchair, but we can get it in the van okay, so we could go for a drive down the coast, find some guest house somewhere, the nurse was saying there's a couple of places would take us, y'know, they don't mind about people being—well, y'know—be nice, getting away for a week or so, by the sea, might do you good, be something to look forward to, anyway.

Might have an ice cream on the way home, you fancy an ice cream? Strawberry cone, be easy enough for you.

Don't suppose you could manage an ice-block, not unless I broke it up into little pieces, and that could get a bit messy. You don't want 'o do wees, or anything, do you?

(DAD buzzes a BUZZER on the arm of his chair.)

JEFF. We, you let me know if you do. I could sit here all day, it's been a prick of a winter. I wonder what's on telly tonight? (*HE sees someone in the distance.*) That's what I like about spring, suddenly everyone busts out into their summer clothes, like that bloke over there in shorts, would've thought it wasn't warm enough for shorts myself, be a bit cool around the knees, but he looks real nice, sexy—Looks a bit like young Greg. Cripes, it is.

(HE tries to make himself look inconspicuous. After a moment, GREG arrives, wearing shorts and boots, pushing a wheelbarrow with plants.)

GREG. G'day, Jeff. Thought it was you.

JEFF. Greg—g'day. Fancy meeting you here.

GREG. I'm working here today, planting. G'day, Mr. Mitchell, remember me? Greg. You not well?

(DAD BUZZES on the arm of the chair.)

JEFF. Dad's had a bit of a stroke.

GREG. That's bad luck, isn't it? Sorry to hear that, Mr. Mitchell.

JEFF. He can't answer or nothing, but he remembers you.

GREG. How can you tell?

JEFF. Oh, well, you work it out. He buzzes on his chair, once for yes, twice for no, and three times for silly.

GREG. Silly?

JEFF. He always used to say that, there's only three possible answers to any question, yes, no and silly.

GREG. He's probably right and all. Saw you from a distance, but I wasn't sure if it was you.

JEFF. I saw you too, didn't recognize you in your shorts. I was having a bit of a perve. You got nice legs.

GREG. You're looking pretty fit yourself.

JEFF. Ah, I need some sun. At least you've got a bit of a tan.

GREG. Only my face and legs. Rest of me's as white as a ghost.

JEFF. Looks all right to me.

GREG. *(Grins appreciatively, then glances at Dad.)* Should we be talking like this, in front of him?

JEFF. He never minded before. You remember what he was like.

GREG. Yeh, but him being sick and all.

JEFF. He's not sick now, and anyway, it makes no odds. What about you? How are things with you?

GREG. Not bad, I've left home.

JEFF. Your folks?

GREG. Dad saw me in town with a couple of friends from the Prinny, and, well, they're a bit obvious, you know? Dad wanted to know all about it when I got home, so I told him.

JEFF. World War Three?

GREG. Mum's been beaut, but Dad—

JEFF. At lease he didn't kill you.

GREG. He kicked me out, lock, stock and barrel. I found a little place of my own. Studio apartment they call it, it's quite nice, but there's hardly room to swing a cat, and it's a bit dear.

JEFF. Would have thought you'd have found some nice friend to move in with.

GREG. Huh. Half my luck. Oh, I meet blokes, but they're all only after one thing, it seems, and it's not everything in life, is it? They never seem very interested in me as a person.

JEFF. Can't understand it.

GREG. Look, I can't stop, the foreman here's a prick. I told him I was going for a leak, but would you like—I mean, we could meet at the pub sometime, have a drink?

JEFF. It's a bit difficult with Dad—

GREG. If you don't want to—

JEFF. Oh no, it's not that, I do, dead set I do, it's just a bit difficult with Dad—

GREG. You've got to have a bit of a life of your own, surely?

(DAD BUZZES urgently.)

JEFF. Yeh, for sure, I do, but—you going for a slash, you say, I need one meself, I'll walk over with you.

GREG. What about Dad?

JEFF. He'll be all right, the brake's on, he can't go anywhere. You be right then, Dad? I'm just going for a walk.

GREG. Nice to see you again, Mr. Mitchell—Dad. Sorry about your—um—hope you feel better soon. I might drop round one Saturday and see you're being looked after properly.

JEFF. That'd be nice of you, Greg, he'd like that. You'd like that, wouldn't you?

GREG. Hooroo, then, Dad. (*HE collects his wheelbarrow.*)

JEFF. Need a hand?

GREG. Nah, I can manage, I'm big and butch. (*Winks.*) Sometimes.

(HE and JEFF move away.)

GREG. Y'know, there's a thing that's been puzzling me. That night at your place, I was a silly little shit that night, sorry about that. But your Dad made some crack about lavender floor polish, and you got a bit funny about it. I've been racking my brains to work out what it was.

JEFF. Ah, that's a bit off, that is, you'd have to be really broad-minded—

(THEY'VE gone.)

DAD. (*Looks at the audience.*) The trouble with having a stroke is that people treat you like a fuckwit afterwards. They do. They stand around talking about you, as if you weren't there. He does, Jeff, he treats me like an imbecile, he can't seem to understand that my mind's going nineteen to the dozen, just like always, but I can't get my body to communicate what I'm thinking. He treats me like I was a little kid. Well. So I am, I suppose. Can't do anything for myself. Can't even go to the lav my myself. I used to enjoy that, just sitting there, reading or dreaming of all the things that I was going to do, one day. Never going to do any of 'em now, of course. But it was always a very private thing, to me, going to the lav. Not any more, with His Nibs fussing around worrying about my motions. You worry about your own bloody motions, I say to meself, but of course, he can't hear me. Doesn't want to hear me, sometimes. Doesn't want to know what I really feel. Likes to put his own interpretation on it, I'm the poor old invalid, and he's the suffering only son who's got to stay home and look after Dad.

Just going for a walk, he must think I'm stupid. I know there's a public convenience in the middle of the park, I know what goes on in some of those places. He says he doesn't do that sort of thing, but he never brings anyone home anymore. Maybe he's ashamed of me, I don't know. How could anyone guess he'd end up like this, doing it in a public lav with Gary of all people, when both of them want more, so much more, plain as the nose on your face.

Is it Gary or Greg? I can't remember. I can't!

Dear God. I didn't want it to end up like this. anything, but this. I didn't even have the chance to say goodbye to him properly. Oh, I'm going to live for years they tell me, God forbid, but it's not the same; in many ways it's as good as being dead. I can't talk to him—communicate—except by buzzing, and that's no way to say goodbye, or even to say thank you.

My mother was nearly eighty and was getting infirm. Mary was a bit younger, but neither of them could look after each other any more, so we all made the decision to split them up, my brother took Mum, and Mary went to a home. It was for their own good. How many times did we tell ourselves that?

We got there about ten in the morning, and they were packed and ready to go, had been for hours probably, sitting in the little sitting room, it was as clean as a new pin, I remember, both dressed in their Sunday best, not talking, just waiting, two human beings in pain, wanting to leave, to get it over with. Mary was crying, not great sobs, just totally miserable, and Gran held her hands, kissed her on the cheeks, twice, but neither of them would let go of their hands. We had to force them apart in the end. They didn't speak or anything, they just wouldn't let go of each other's hands.

(The memory distresses him)

We drove Gran away and she didn't say a word, didn't speak for days just sat in her new bedroom with her suitcase full of memories. A lifetime of memories in one little suitcase. Three months later we heard that Mary had passed away. Mum took it on the chin, it was like she'd been expecting it, but it was all downhill for my mother after that. I don't think it was that she wanted to go, so much as she couldn't see a reason to stay. She died one night in her sleep soon after, and I never had a chance, or the guts, to ask her the thing I really wanted to know.

I've always wanted to know what they said to each other that last night, lying in that great old brass bed, knowing it was for the last time, knowing they'd never see each other again, knowing that they were being taken away to different places to die.

How do you say thank you for forty years of love, what words could you possibly find? And by that time they were both as deaf as posts, so did they lie there shouting their love and their goodbyes, to one another? Did they find comfort in the idea that they'd meet again soon in the next life? But considering what they'd being doing in that same bed for the last forty years, they couldn't even be certain of that, could they? For forty years, they'd shared everything together, the most intimate places of their bodies and their hearts. They didn't want to leave each other, they were being forced apart. But how on earth did they say goodbye? I can't imagine what they might have said.

So I don't know what I would have said to Jeffrey, if I'd known the stroke was going to happen, and I was gong to be left like this. I don't know what I'd say to him if I'd been told I was going to die, but I know I would have said something, and now I'll never find out what it was.

Well, that's about it, you might as well go home now, nothing's going to happen now. Oh maybe in a few years time, when I'm gone, he'll find somebody, if only out of sheer bloody loneliness, but it won't be love, because by then he'll have forgotten how, and I can't think of a worse thing to happen to a human being than that.

I suppose some of you were hoping for a happy ending, in which case you've done your money. He'll be back in a few minutes looking like a cat who's just had a bowl of cream, and we'll sit here for a while, then we'll go home and he'll cook fish or lasagna because he thinks I like it, and I am sick to bloody death of fish, and lasagna. And I'll resent him, because he isn't taking advantage of his life, and he'll resent me, because he'll think I'm stopping him taking advantage of life, and we might even end up hating each other. Not a very nice thing to look forward to, is it? Sometimes I think it would be easier all round if I just—ended it. After all, what have I got to look forward to, except a few years of him cooking fish or lasagna and wiping my bum, which is not exactly the plan I had for my later years. Nor for his. But there's nothing I can do, I can't even turn on the gas my myself and anyway, our house is all electric. Pathetic, isn't it? I can't even kill myself.

(JEFF comes back looking like a cat that's just had a bowl of cream. DAD returns to his "stroke" state.)

JEFF. You all right then, Dad?

(DAD BUZZES the arm of his chair.)

JEFF. (*Somewhat self-conscious about his absence.*) Sorry I was a while, we had a nice chat, that's all. I'll read to you for a bit, want me to read to you?

(DAD BUZZES twice.)

JEFF. No? What do you want to do then, eh? Just sit here for a bit? Listen to the flowers grow? (*HE dreams his dream for a moment, in the calm of the spring day, then HE glances at his father.*) Hope you don't mind too much about just now, Dad, with Greg. Could've knocked me down with a feather, seeing him here. I couldn't believe me luck, though I suppose it's only natural, him being a gardener. I just wanted to talk to him, and that's all we did, cross my heart.

And I couldn't help meself. I asked him home for tea one night, thinking he'd just say, oh yeah, that'd be nice, and walk off. But like you're always saying, you don't ask you don't get. Could've knocked me down with a feather when he said would tomorrow be all right. Yeh, ripper, I said. Could've knocked me down with a feather. I was a bit worried about you, how he'd feel about you, your table manners aren't exactly top deck these days, and you do tend to fart rather a lot, but he just shrugged and said, well, that's life, isn't it?

So he's coming for tea tomorrow night. Hope you don't mind, Dad, but you seemed to get on all right with him last time, and he says he'll bring a couple of poetry books and read you some if you like, be a bit of a change from the telly for you, wouldn't it? And, well, he said he'd bring his toothbrush, too, I mean, that's making it fairly plain isn't it, he might even stay the night. Course, he winked when he said it, so he was probably joking, about the toothbrush, but at least he's coming for tea, that's if he shows up, so if you do mind, Dad, that's tough, and that's all there is about it.

I like him, Dad, I really do. He says he likes me. Looked really sexy in those shorts. There's probably dozens of blokes fancy him, he could take his pick. Still, I suppose, he's not that perfect. Bit chunky round the bum. I like 'em that way meself, but lots don't.

I'm not gonna rush things, though, just play it as it comes. Joe Cool, this time, you watch me. Not too cool, don't want him thinking I'm not interested, just, well—I'll try and be me, whoever that is.

I'll cook something nice. What'll I cook? Lasagna? You like that don't yer? Still, we have it quite a lot. I could do a roast. A nice roast pork? With really crispy crackling. But I suppose that's a bit rich for you, Dad. Steak. That's it, I'll blow a few bob, get a really nice piece of steak. Couple of

T-bones, that's the go, and there's asparagus in the shops already, I saw some the other day.

Sorry, Dad, I meant three T-bones, of course. Though I don't suppose you'd be too keen on 'em, would you? Could be a bit difficult for you to chew. Fish, I'll get you a piece of fish. We'll have T-bones, you can have a nice bit of flounder, that all right?

What's up, Dad? What's the matter, mate? You're crying. Ah, come on, it can't be that bad, whatever it is. Here, come on, dry your eyes, it'll be all right. (*HE wipes his father's eyes with his own hanky.*) Don't, Dad, please stop. Breaks me up to see you like this. Come on, here— (*HE takes his father into his arms, and hugs him hard.*) There's nothing to get yourself all upset about, I'm here. I'll always be here, I promise.

Is it Greg, don't you want him to come to tea? I won't I'll stop him if you want me too, I've got his phone number—

(But his FATHER is BUZZING, urgently.)

JEFF. Is that what it is? Tell me, come on, one buzz for yes, two buzzes for no.

(One BUZZ.)

JEFF. You want me to cancel it?

(Two BUZZES.)

JEFF. No, you don't want me to?

(One BUZZ.)

JEFF. Yes. That's what I thought. (*HE hugs his father.*) You all right? You sure? Silly old bastard, aren't you? Getting yourself worked up over things. There's nothing to worry about, Dad, I promise yer. (*HE smiles at the sun.*) Not a worry in the world. (*And at his dad.)* Turned out real nice, after all, didn't it? I wonder if he'll show up?

(DAD throws his eyes to heaven.
THEY sit there, in the sunlight. The father and the son.)

COSTUME PLOT

HARRY

Scene 1
Brown pants
Blue and white striped shirt
Brown suspenders
White undershirt
Light tan Hush Puppies
Light tan socks
Watch
Wallet

Scene 2
Burgundy pajamas
Burgundy and navy blue robe
Light tan slippers

Scene 3
Khaki shorts
Light blue shirt
Light tan socks
Dark brown shoes

Scene 4
Navy pants
Black belt
Repeat scene 3 shirt
Blue tie
Tan checked sports jacket
Repeat scene 3 socks and shoes

Scene 5
Repeat scene 4 pants, belt, shirt, shoes and socks
Burgundy windbreaker jacket

JEFF
Scene 1
Footy shorts
Footy shirt
Long white socks (distressed)
Blue sneakers
Cleated shoes

Towel

Maroon T-shirt
Pink shirt
Light blue jeans
Dark blue jeans
Brown belt
Dusty blue socks
Dessert boots
Watch

Scene 2
Repeat end scene 1

Scene 3
Navy T-shirt (distressed)
Navy work pants
White sports socks

Scene 5
Light blue work shirt
Yellow T-shirt
Repeat scene 3 navy work pants
Black belt
White socks
Repeat scene 1 blue sneakers
Handkerchief

GREG
Scene 2
Black pants
Black belt
Blue shirt
Black cardigan
Brown and grey socks
Brown shoes

Scene 5
Brown shorts
3-button long sleeve brown T-shirt
Red and brown athletic socks
Work boots

JOYCE
Scene 4
Lilac dress
Bone shoes
Bone belt
Bone purse
White shawl; Single pearl necklace
2 bracelets (1 gold; 1 bone),;Pearl button earrings

PROPERTY PLOT

PRESHOW PRESET
Onstage
Pouf—on: 3 porn magazines
magazines
newspapers

Cabinet—on:
framed photograph of Jeff
framed photograph of Harry's wedding
lamp
Sir Richard Burton book

Bar—on:
Irish Cream
Cointreau
Whisky
6 highball glasses
4 cordial glasses

Dining table—on:
ketchup
napkins

Small table—on:
phone
ashtray
matches

Coffee table—on:
ashtray
matches

newspaper
book

Off Right:
2 plates (scene 1)
2 forks (scene 1)
2 knives (scene 1)
7 Foster beers (scene 1-2; scene 2-5)
Pan of lasagna with spatula (scene 1)
Bowl of peas with spoon (scene 1)
Bowl of mashed potatoes with spoon (scene 1)
3 dish towels (scene 1)
ice (scene 2)
plate with 2 mince meat tarts (scene 3)
1 highball glass (scene 3)
2 wine glasses (scene 4)
wheelchair (scene 5)
blanket (scene 5)
wheelbarrow (scene 5)
3 books (scene 5)

RUNNING
Scene 1 to Scene 2
Strike: from dining table—
1 plate
1 knife
1 fork
1 spoon
1 beer
bowl of mashed potatoes
bowl of peas
pan of lasagna

from coffee table— dish towel
from bar— dish towel
from cabinet Sir Richard Burton book

Intermission

Set onstage: Christmas tree
box of tree ornaments including a fairy
Set on coffee table: highball glass
ornament hooks
joint

Scene 3 to Scene 4
Strike: Christmas tree
box of ornaments
whisky
plate with mince meat tarts
2 highball glasses
ashtray
matches
joint

Scene 4 to Scene 5
Pivot coffee table to bench position
Set: books on bench
Strike: 3 porn magazines
1 wine glass
2 cordial glasses

THE NORMAL HEART

(Advanced Groups.) Drama. Larry Kramer. 8m., 1f. Unit set. The New York Shakespeare Festival had quite a success with this searing drama about public and private indifference to the Acquired Immune Deficiency Syndrome plague, commonly called AIDS, and about one man's lonely fight to wake the world up to the crisis. The play has subsequently been produced to great acclaim in London and Los Angeles. Brad Davis originated the role of Ned Weeks, a gay activist enraged at the foot-dragging of both elected public officials and the gay community itself regarding AIDS. Ned not only is trying to save the world from itself, he also must confront the personal toll of AIDS when his lover contracts the disease and ultimately dies. This is more than just a gay play about a gay issue. This is a public health issue which affects all of us. He further uses this theatrical platform to plead with gay brethren to stop thinking of themselves only in terms of their sexuality, and that rampant sexual promiscuity will not only almost guarantee that they will contract AIDS; it is also bad for them as human beings. "An angry, unremitting and gripping piece of political theatre."—N.Y. Daily News. "Like the best social playwright, Kramer produces a cross-fire of life and death energies that illuminate the many issues and create a fierce and moving human drama."—Newsweek. $4.50. (Royalty $60-$40.) Slightly Restricted. **(#788)**

A QUIET END

(Adult Groups.) Drama. Robin Swados. 5m. Int. Three men—a schoolteacher, an aspiring jazz pianist and an unemployed actor—have been placed in a run-down Manhattan apartment. All have lost their jobs, all have been shunned by their families, and all have AIDS. They have little in common, it seems, apart from their slowing evolving, albeit uneasy, friendships with each other, and their own mortality. The interaction of the men with a psychiatrist (heard but not seen throughout the course of the play) and the entrance into this arena of the ex-lover of one of the three—seemingly healthy, yet unsure of his future—opens up the play's true concerns: the meaning of friendship, loyalty and love. By celebrating the lives of four men who, in the face of death, become more fearlessly life-embracing instead of choosing the easier path to a quiet end, the play explores the human side of the AIDS crisis, examining how we choose to lead our lives—and how we choose to end them. "The play, as quiet in its message as in its ending, gets the measure of pain and love in a bitter-chill climate."—N.Y. Post. "In a situation that will be recognizable to most gay people, it is the chosen family rather than the biological family, that has become important to these men. Robin Swados has made an impressive debut with *A Quiet End* by accurately representing the touching relationships in such a group."—N.Y. Native. (Royalty $60-$40.) Music Note: Samuel French, Inc. can supply a cassette tape of music from the original New York production, composed by Robin Swados, upon receipt of a refundable deposit of $25.00, (tape must be returned within one week from the close of your production) and a rental fee of $15.00 **per performance**. Use of this music in productions is **optional**. **(#19017)**

ESTABLISHED PRICE

By Dennis McIntyre

(Little Theatre.) Comedy. 4m. Int. This timely new comedy by the author of *Split Second* and *Modigliani* has had two major successful regional productions, and is now available for the first time. It is a comedy of white-collar angst in this age of corporate takeovers, focusing on the predicament of middle-aged managers who suddenly find themselves out of a job—like just above everyone else—when the company for whom they have worked most of their working lives is taken over and dismantled by a corporate raider. True, each is provided with a handsome "golden parachute"—but this is small recompense—as well as an inadequate replacement for—their jobs, which have become their identity. The central character, Frank Daniels (played in Philadelphia by Kenneth McMillan and at the Long Wharf Theatre by Jason Robards) is the former general counsel for the cannibalized corporation—and he does not intend to go gently into the good night of his forced retirement. He refuses to pack, tears up the office, and tries to get his fellow executives to decline their golden parachutes as a protest over what has happened to them. Naturally, they think he's crazy, which he may just be—and they certainly do not intend to give back their checks. In the end, even Frank capitulates, and pockets the check. He may be crazy, but he's not stupid! "Taut and heart-felt."—Phila. Daily News. "Our playwrights are supposed to do this for us. They are supposed to bring into the open whatever it is that is eating away at us, as Arthur Miller once did and as few playwrights have done since. Now comes Dennis McIntyre, locating the trouble and lifting it from the financial pages of our newspaper to put it in the context of our lives. His play about a corporate takeover is a searchlight revealing the latest alarming shift of the national energy away from people and toward the bottom line."—Phila. Inquirer. "[A] knowing and extremely timely new play."—N.Y. Times.. **(#7085)**

NATIONAL ANTHEMS

By Dennis McIntyre

(Little Theatre.) Comic Drama. 2m., 1f. Int. Tom Berenger, Kevin Spacey and Mary McDonnell starred in the acclaimed Long Wharf Theatre production of this insightful, hard-hitting new play from the author of *Modigliani*, *Split Second* and *Established Price*. We are in the sumptuous home of Arthur and Leslie Reed, who have had a party that evening for their neighbors. It is very late , and all the guests have gone home, when one final guest arrives, a fireman named Ben Cook, a working man not, shall we say, from the Reeds' socio-economic background. Nonetheless, the Reeds play gracious hosts—until, that is, things get nasty, as Ben increasingly shows his desperation about everything his life lacks in the way of material comforts, status and personal pride. Eventually, the two men get drunk as skunks and come to blows, in this apt parable about America's love-affair with materialism. "Topical, perverse and funny."—Variety. "Profane, smart and disturbingly funny . . . with an acuteness that's as up-to-date as this morning's newspaper headlines."—Rochester Times-Union. "Excoriating assault on traditional American values. Mr. McIntyre demonstrates his visceral sense of theatricality as well as his own state-of-the-heart awareness of contemporary behavior."—N.Y. Times. **(#15982)**

THE FILM SOCIETY
Jon Robin Baitz
(Little Theatre) Dramatic comedy
4m., 2f. Various ints. (may be unit set)

Imagine the best of Simon Gray crossed with the best of Athol Fugard. The New York critics lavished praise upon this wonderful play, calling Mr. Baitz a major new voice in our theatre. *The Film Society*, set in South Africa, is *not* about the effects of apartheid—at least. overtly. Blenheim is a provincial private school modeled on the second-rate British education machine. It is 1970, a time of complacency for everyone but Terry. a former teacher at Blenheim, who has lost his job because of his connections with Blacks (he invited a Black priest to speak at commencement). Terry tries to involve Jonathan, another teacher at the school and the central character in this play; but Jonathan cares only about his film society, which he wants to keep going at all costs—even if it means programming only safe, non-objectionable, films. When Jonathan's mother, a local rich lady, promises to donate a substantial amount of money to Blenheim if Jonathan is made Headmaster, he must finally choose which side he is on: Terry's or The Establishment's. "Using the school as a microcosm for South Africa, Baitz explores the psychological workings of repression in a society that has to kill its conscience in order to persist in a course of action it knows enough to abhor but cannot afford to relinquish."—New Yorker. "What distinguishes Mr. Baitz' writing, aside from its manifest literacy, is its ability to embrace the ambiguities of political and moral dilemmas that might easily be reduced to blacks and whites."—N.Y. Times. "A beautiful, accomplished play . . . things I thought I was a churl still to value or expect—things like character, plot and theatre dialogue—really do matter."—N.Y. Daily News. **(#8123)**

THE SUBSTANCE OF FIRE
Jon Robin Baitz
(Little Theatre.) Drama
3m., 2f. 2 Ints.

Isaac Geldhart, the scion of a family-owned publisher in New York which specializes in scholarly books, suddenly finds himself under siege. His firm is under imminent threat of a corporate takeover, engineered by his own son, Aaron, who watches the bottom line and sees the firm's profitability steadily declining. Aaron wants to publish a trashy novel which will certainly bring in the bucks; whereas Isaac wants to go on publishing worthy scholarly efforts such as his latest project, a multi-volume history of Nazi medical experiments during the Holocaust. Aaron has the bucks to effectively wrench control of the company from his father—or, rather, he has the yen (Japanese businessmen are backing him). What he needs are the votes of the other minority shareholders: his brother Martin and sister Sarah. Like Aaron, they have lived their lives under the thumb of Isaac's imperiousness; and, reluctantly, they agree to side with Aaron against the old man. In the second act, we are back in the library of Isaac's townhouse, a few years later. Isaac has been forcibly retired and has gotten so irascible and eccentric that he may possibly be *non compos mentis*. His children think so, which is why they have asked a psychiatric social worker from the court to interview Isaac to judge his competence. Isaac, who has survived the Holocaust and the death of his wife to build an important publishing company from scratch, must now face his greatest challenge—to persuade Marge Hackett that he is sane. "A deeply compassionate play."—N.Y. Times. "A remarkably intelligent drama. Baitz assimilates and refracts this intellectual history without stinting either on heart or his own original vision."—N.Y. Newsday. **(#21379)**